ETHEREUM

THE DEFINITIVE QUICK & EASY

BLUEPRINT TO UNDERSTAND AND

PROFIT WITH ETHEREUM

Also by Victor Finch

~~~~~~~~~~~~

Data Analytics For Beginners: Your Ultimate Guide To Learn and Master Data Analytics. Get Your Business Intelligence Right – Accelerate Growth and Close More Sales

Victor's Insider Tip: Sign up below link to buy or sell Bitcoin, Ethereum, Litecoin and Get $10 free for every $100 transaction. Only available with below link.

https://www.auvapress.com/victor-shares/coinbase

See more books: **https://www.auvapress.com/books**

Leave a review on Amazon:

https://www.auvapress.com/amazon-review/ethereum

GET YOUR EARLY GROWTH NOW!

ETHEREUM

THE DEFINITIVE QUICK & EASY BLUEPRINT TO
UNDERSTAND AND PROFIT WITH ETHEREUM

VICTOR FINCH

AUVA PRESS

Trademarks:

FIRST EDITION

ISBN-13: 978-1-5487-8437-9
ISBN-10: 1-5487-8437-0

Editor: Kit White
Cover Designer: Terrence Reese

To my loved ones and friends, friendship and to my family,
who make my world more purposeful and meaningful

CONTENTS

PREFACE 7

Chapter 1 Introduction To Ethereum...........................11

What is Ethereum? 13

Brief history of Ethereum growth..............................16

Ethereum's vision 18

Differences between Ethereum and Bitcoin 21

Pros and cons of Ethereum 23

Which is better for investment and has more potential

for monetary growth?..25

Which is better in technology?..................................26

Which is more popular? 27

Which is easier to mine? 28

Chapter 2 Technology Engine behind Ethereum............29

Ethereum Technology stack and the big picture 30

Ethereum Supporting Protocols 30

Scripting language 33

Ethereum Transactions 34

The Ethereum Blockchain 36

Consensus Algorithms...39

Ethereum Mining...42

Ethereum Basic Hardware and Software 44

Ethereum mining tools...48

Setting up the mining process 50

Ethereum mining profitability calculator 55

Ethereum Virtual Machine (EVM) 56

Ethereum Supporting Protocols 62

Chapter 3 Ethereum Use Cases 68

Smart Contracts 69

DAOs 71

Dapps 73

Chapter 4 Ethereum Investment Basics 77

The concept of Ether 78

Ethereum Trading 82

Ethereum Wallet 83

Ethereum security 85

Chapter 5 **Ethereum Key Players and Technical**

Infrastructure 88

Developer Leads 89

The Ethereum Foundation 90

Decentralized Projects 90

Startups 91

Chapter 6 The Future of Ethereum 92

CONCLUSION 98

FURTHER RESOURCES **101**

NOTES...**102**

ABOUT THE AUTHOR..**104**

PREFACE

When the Bitcoin crypto currency system was launched in 2009, it triggered a social and technological revolution that has continued to send ripples across a horde of industries. From the financial sector to the healthcare industry, the list of companies that have jumped on the Bitcoin bandwagon continues to skyrocket.

Bitcoin was the first technology that allowed us to send money across the Internet in a secure manner without censorship and any fear of fraud. Besides its initial applications in the financial industry, other technology enthusiasts saw promising value in the Bitcoin powering technology: Blockchain. As a result, what started off as a revolutionary approach to transferring money also held the potential to completely transform the web.

Amidst all the hype that Bitcoin generated, there were a couple of limitations, the most vital one being the fact that the system wasn't designed to transmit more than a few KBs per transaction. Besides, the system wasn't able to perform computations that didn't fit into its limited scripting language. In fact, Satoshi Nakamoto—the mysterious inventor of Bitcoin—believed that placing a caveat on Bitcoin's functionality would significantly enhance its security. However, the result has in fact been disastrous. As the volume of transactions increased, the system continued to slow down, therefore, jamming the transactions.

Vitalik Buterin, the inventor of the Ethereum technology, visualized things a bit differently. He envisioned the Ethereum technology as a "World Computer"—one that fits the description of a Virtual Machine perfectly. When combined with a Turing-complete language (Solidity), a token (ETH) and fuel (gas), Ethereum can power every transaction on its network, eliminating the bottlenecks witnessed in the Bitcoin technology.

This combination has led to the development of more complex and programmatic systems that couldn't even be envisioned with the Bitcoin technology.

But what exactly is Ethereum?

Well, this guidebook explores all the ins and outs of Ethereum to provide you with the details of the system. Specifically, you'll learn about how Ethereum is different from Bitcoin, the building blocks of Ethereum, the cases in which Ethereum can be used, the basics of investment, such as how to synchronize your Ethereum wallet and the technical infrastructure of Ethereum network.

Are you ready?

Chapter 1

Introduction To Ethereum

Welcome to the world of Ethereum technology! This chapter introduces you to the world of the so-called crypto currencies and gives you the big picture of Ethereum systems.

Are you ready?

Before we start, we will need to answer the following question: "What is a crypto currency system?"

Well, a crypto currency—sometimes called virtual currency—is digital money. However, unlike the fiat money, such as the dollars and sterling pounds that you're used to, crypto currencies are not regulated by central banks or government institutions. A community of Blockchain developers manages them.

So, why are crypto currency systems becoming a fad these days?

It's simple.

The exponential growth of the internet has completely changed how the purchase and sale of goods take place. With great online marketplaces such as eBay, Amazon, and other web stores, all you have to do is to conduct research about the product or service you'd like to buy from the comfort of your house. Once you've settled on one, you simply need to use your credit card to complete the purchasing process.

In other words, how commerce is performed has shifted from brick and mortar shops to online marketplaces. Today, buyers are more likely to buy goods from online by using online payment systems such as PayPal, Skrill, and Payoneer, rather than from brick and mortar stores. But I'm sure we all know the challenges that come with using these systems.

Besides requiring you to have a valid email address and bank account, these systems are extremely bureaucratic when it comes to the processing of transactions. In fact, if you forget your password or if suspicious activity is detected, your account can be frozen without prior warning! Furthermore, the transaction costs are extremely high.

Meanwhile, the crypto currency systems flip the conventional payment systems on their head.

You can use a virtual currency the same way you use cash. It is just like having cash but rather than buying goods and services from brick and mortar shops, you'll now be using the virtual currency system to purchase goods and services from online storefronts as they accept it as a form of payment.

Now that you've understood crypto currency systems and why they are popular, what's next?

Let's now dive deeper to learn more about Ethereum.

What is Ethereum?

Simply put, Ethereum is a form of crypto currency. Just like Bitcoin, Ethereum provides a decentralized network that executes peer-to-peer transactions using a crypto currency called Blockchain technology. However, Bitcoin has been around for much longer as compared to Ethereum (since 2009 when it was conceived by Satoshi Nakamoto).

Bitcoin is commonly used as a store of value and has provided a sneak preview for the public to comprehend the concept of digital currencies. Ethereum is slightly different from Bitcoin in the sense that it permits the development of smart contracts—highly programmable digital money—that allow various parties to conduct business transactions so long as certain conditions have been met.

Imagine a situation where you want to send money to your seller after buying goods from him/her. If you don't have cash, you will have to use the banking system where you'll write a check or use online payment gateways such as PayPal and Skrill. In both cases, you'll be forced to employ the use of third parties such as merchants, lawyers or even escrow services that will make the transaction process pointlessly slow and expensive.

With Ethereum, only a piece of code is required to automatically transfer home ownership to the buyer and the money to the seller once the deal is agreed upon. Furthermore, there is no need for a third party to execute the contract on your behalf. The potential for these self-executing codes is indeed remarkable.

Think of the numerous apps that act as third-party systems, which link those with the same ideas such as Uber, eBay, Airbnb and many others. Truth be told, many of today's centralized apps can be developed in a decentralized approach similar to that of Ethereum.

With decentralization, single points of failures and centralized control in a network can be eliminated, making internal collisions and external attacks nearly impossible. These apps could also phase out the middlemen and other third parties in transactions, therefore, lowering the costs for the user.

In a sense, Ethereum can also be regarded as "the next Internet."

The Internet is commonly known as a single construct with a collection of the web of protocols and rule sets (TCP/IP) that work together to power complex communication and collaboration of business processes. Similarly, Ethereum and its underlying Blockchain technology provide more public, permission-less Blockchain protocols that can be enhanced to become the "internet of value."

With such public utility, Ethereum can provide a layered architecture that expands the Internet of Information—or the Internet as we currently know of— to deliver all services, be it financial or non-financial.

Ethereum and its underlying Blockchain technology can decentralize transactions and minimize bottlenecks of establishing trust in the digital world. First launched in 2014, Ethereum is seen as both a realization for the future—by providing an internet of value—as well as a solution to the limitations found in Bitcoin.

Brief history of Ethereum growth

From a historical perspective, Ethereum can be viewed as an outgrowth of a philosophical subset of the Bitcoin community that sought to develop an additional functionality to the network without generating a new blockchain. This journey began in January 2014 when Vitalik Buterin formally launched

Ethereum at the North American Bitcoin Conference in Florida, USA.

Around the same time, Vitalik began to work with Dr. Gavin Wood, and they then co-founded the Ethereum Foundation, a legal entity that manages both the legal and marketing efforts of Ethereum. In April 2014, Gavin published the Ethereum Yellow Paper that provided the technical specifications for the Ethereum Virtual Machine (EVM).

Following the detailed specifications in the Yellow Paper, today, Ethereum clients have been implemented in seven programming languages, namely C++, Go, Python, Java, JavaScript, Haskell and Rust. In a bid to kick-start a community of developers, miners, and Ethereum investors, the Ethereum Foundation conducted a presale of more than 60 million Ethers (digital tokens).

This marketing campaign turned out to be a major success for the Ethereum Foundation, earning them more than $18 million in just 42 days. It is currently the fifth largest crowdfunding campaign in history.

As a result of the success of the marketing campaign, Buterin and Wood co-opted Wilcke to help them focus on development. They set up another legal entity called ETH DEV, whose primary purpose was to direct and oversee the process of Ethereum development. To keep up with the changes in development and community engagement, they improved the proof of concept algorithm to boost its security.

The Ethereum system went live on June 30, 2015, slightly more than a year and a half after the first publication of Vitalik Buterin's Whitepaper. The result of dozens, if not hundreds of programmers', engineers', and scientists' hard work was that Ethereum culminated in its Frontier release. Initially meant as a beta version, even today, Ethereum developers continue to flock to the network to create a whole horde of complex applications.

Ethereum's vision

Ethereum can be seen as an attempt to apply the mistakes learned from the Bitcoin's decentralized, global cryptographic systems to challenges beyond the value exchange. Instead of disintermediating third parties in e-commerce, Ethereum helped in envisioning how eliminating other traditional arbitrators of trust could promote a new wave of application development.

Let me give an example to illustrate the vision of Ethereum.

I'm sure all of us have accounts, be it bank accounts or social media accounts such as Twitter and Facebook. We all trust our banks to keep our money safe. Otherwise, we wouldn't bother depositing money in that account. Similarly, when you upload your profile picture to your Facebook or Twitter portal, you assume that the picture will be kept safe.

Even as a developer, when submitting your app to the app store, you need to be guaranteed that no one will have it removed. With Ethereum, we simply seek to enable the creation of similar Internet services while restoring the control of personal information and funds to users.

At a time when many Blockchain platforms were being developed with the same concept as Bitcoin, Ethereum envisioned the innovation of apps in four areas:

- *Crypto currency issuance*. Buterin positioned Ethereum as a financial platform that would allow thousands and millions of digital currencies to work on the same network, with the sole aim of being an "economic democracy".
- *Decentralized autonomous organizations (DAOS).* Buterin envisioned how the new forms of crypto currency entities could be developed to manage shared resources under a set of rules and conditions enshrined in a piece of code managed by collective decisions from multiple stakeholders.
- *Smart contracts*. New contracts could be built on Ethereum as pieces of codes instead of being enforced through a traditional legal system.
- *Smart property*. Buterin envisioned an entirely different definition of the property which would expand with concepts of cryptographic and Blockchain-based tokens that serve as representations of the real-world assets, such as museum passes and tickets.

Differences between Ethereum and Bitcoin

The Ethereum systems have continued to receive in-depth news coverage ever since its launch. The apparent after-effect of this growing recognition has been its relentless comparison to Bitcoin—the first virtual currency that was invented in 2009. In fact, at face value, the two systems may appear similar.

Even though they share a common objective, that is to create an open currency that allows every user to use it without permission from a regulator, their differences are multifold. Here are some differences between Ethereum and Bitcoin:

- In Ethereum the block time (also known as the time required to record a transaction successfully) has been set to 14 to 15 seconds. Whereas in Bitcoin, the block time is 10 minutes. Therefore, Ethereum transactions are much faster as compared to Bitcoin transactions. To achieve faster transactions, Ethereum relies on Ghost Protocol.
- The economic model of Ethereum is slightly different from that of Bitcoin. Ethereum does not halve the economic rewards after four years. This means that you'll receive the same amount of Ether each year. However, in Bitcoin, the economic returns are halved every

four years. When it comes to reserve side of the digital currency, there's no limit in Ethereum. As a matter of fact, the amount of Ether that will be circulated is limitless.

- Ethereum has a slightly different method for obtaining the costing of transactions that depends on the computational complexity, bandwidth and other needs of the transaction such as storage capacities in what is commonly called Gas. On the other hand, Bitcoin transactions compete on equal ground.

- Ethereum has its own Virtual Machine (Turing complete internal code) that increases its computing power and reduces the time needed for its transactions. With Bitcoin, there is no Virtual Machine to achieve the same form of flexibility as Ethereum.

- Ethereum was crowdfunded while Bitcoin was simply released. Hence, early miners own most of the Bitcoins that will ever be mined. With Ethereum, miners will own 50% of the Ethers in the fifth year since its launch.

- Ethereum discourages the centralized pool mining through its Ghost protocol that rewards the stale blocks. Therefore, there is no merit to being in an Ethereum pool regarding block propagation.

- Bitcoin has a fixed limit of approximately 21 million Bitcoins. It is expected that the last block will be mined at around 2140. Furthermore, the early miners of Bitcoin possess the majority of the coins that will be exploited in the future. This is in contrast to Ethereum which was crowd-funded. Also, 50% of its Ether is projected to be owned by all of its miners within the next five years.

- Ethereum uses a memory hard hashing algorithm called Ethash that prevents the use of ASICS and encourages decentralized mining in Ethereum.

Pros and cons of Ethereum

It's often said that "Ethereum is oil while Bitcoin is gold." What does this statement imply about the pros and cons of each system? Let's dive in and explore.

Let's begin by exploring Ethereum.

Ethereum is essentially a Virtual Machine (EVM) that is decentralized and can provide cloud computing services with a 100% uptime. If you want to run any code reliably, securely and anonymously without the involvement of third parties, then running the code on EVM makes sense. It not only opens up a vast range of possibilities for app development but also creates secure apps that people can trust to manage their operations.

To execute your code on the Ethereum blockchain, all you need to do is to pay for the gas each time the Ethereum code script runs. This not only generates an economic use for the Ether but also deters infinite looping codes that could otherwise be used to attack EVM systems.

What about Bitcoin?

There is no coding on the Bitcoin Blockchain. Rather, developers create "sidechains" that operate off of the main Bitcoin Blockchain, leaving the Blockchain untouched. This means that you can't use Bitcoin in the same manner that you could use Ethereum. Therefore, the merits of Ethereum mentioned above cannot be applied to Bitcoin.

If you were to ask the following question: "Can Bitcoin do anything that Ethereum can't?" The answer would be that as it stands now, Ethereum can perform virtually everything that Bitcoin can. In fact, you can generate your own version of Bitcoin on the Ethereum Blockchain. Going further, you can even develop entirely new crypto currencies using the Ethereum

Blockchain. However, the main differentiators that will always fall in Bitcoin's favor are:

- The Bitcoin currency system is deflationary. Just like gold, Bitcoin has a limited supply in existence, making it an incredible store of value that can be easily transacted as compared to other crypto currencies.
- The network effect. The power of the network effect can't be overemphasized in the adoption of Bitcoin. Since it is extremely unlikely that another currency will bust the Bitcoin currency overnight, the currency will always tip its "first mover advantage" to out-maneuver other crypto currencies since it has gained a wider acceptance and adoption.

Which is better for investment and has more potential for monetary growth?

Strictly speaking, the two crypto currencies provide much-needed support to each another. Now, as crypto currencies gain acceptance in a variety of uses, more people will begin to experience the real value for monetary growth. Also, the adoption of either currency doesn't mean that transfers between Ether and Bitcoin will be seamless.

However, when it comes to the debate between Ethereum and Bitcoin, the market has always favored an open, flexible and scalable system that can overcome individual issues. Personally, I will vouch for Ethereum because of the following reasons:

- Bitcoin has a fixed supply in existence, making it an incredible store of value that can be easily transacted compared to other crypto currencies. But therein lies the disadvantage— no possibility allows no growth. In fact, Bitcoin has a fixed limit of approximately 21 million Bitcoins that will be exhausted in 2140. On the other hand, Ether is projected to be owned by all its miners by 2021.
- Ethereum is faster compared to Bitcoin. The block time has been set from 14 to 15 seconds using a Ghost protocol while that of Bitcoin is 10 minutes. Therefore, Ethereum transactions are faster when compared to Bitcoin transactions.

Which is better in technology?

Obviously, Ethereum has better technology than the Bitcoin network. Even though both technologies rely on Blockchain, Ethereum is more than a crypto currency. It features the smart contracts, the Ethereum Virtual Machine and the Ether for peer-to-peer contracts. Besides providing a larger block size, Ethereum also speeds up the rate at which transactions can be conducted.

The Bitcoin system wasn't designed to transmit more than a few KBs of data per transaction. Furthermore, it isn't able to perform computations that don't fit into its limited scripting language. When you compare the differences between Ethereum's and Bitcoin's Block size and computational power, Ethereum is indeed more powerful.

Which is more popular?

At the moment, Bitcoin is still attractive when compared to Ethereum. However, this will only be temporary due to the "network effect" that Bitcoin has generated. The Bitcoin currency has continued to outshine Ethereum because of its "first mover advantage". Hence, it is extremely unlikely that another currency will bust it overnight. But going forward, Ethereum will definitely gain more ground because of its promising and improved capabilities.

Which is easier to mine?

Undoubtedly, Ethereum is easier to mine than Bitcoin. However, it may not be worth it unless you invest significant sums of resources and switch between the crypto currencies to obtain the best out of all of them. You can do this either by saving them for future uses or trading them on the crypto currencies stocks.

Instead, your best bet is to create a multi-mining pool that you can easily mine. You can also switch between the coins depending on which currency is more lucrative that day. The value of Ethereum mining is as risky as investing. Therefore, you have to figure out all the mining requirements before you jump into it.

Chapter 2

Technology Engine behind Ethereum

Just like the Internet, Ethereum isn't just one thing, but is instead a sum of many components. This chapter explores the building blocks behind the Ethereum. Now, let's get started.

Ethereum Technology stack and the big picture

The Ethereum system contains a non-exhaustive list of components with cryptographic tokens, the address system, miners or network of validators, consensus algorithm, a blockchain ledger, the Ethereum, Virtual Machine, programming languages scripts and complex economic structures.

The diagram below summarizes the Ethereum technology stack:

Mist browser		
Decentralized apps (Dapps)		
Swarm (storage)	Whisper (Messaging)	Oracles
Hardware Clients		

Ethereum Supporting Protocols

At the bottom of the Ethereum technology is the hardware system. For your hardware system to support Ethereum, you'll need fast processing power with the following specifications:

- CPU. When selecting the CPU, you should go for the bare minimum to deal with high computations.
- RAM. You should have a computer with a minimum RAM of 4GB.
- GPU. Ethereum computations are carried out within the GPU. Therefore, a powerful GPU that has high computational capabilities will be your best bet.
- Hard drive. For the hard disk, using an SSD is critical.

More details on the hardware system specifications will be provided in a later chapter.

The second layer of the Ethereum stack technology comprises of software and their accompanying protocols. These rules support the development and growth of Ethereum by complimenting the network to make the components run more efficiently. The most common protocols at this layer are:

- Whisper. Whisper is a communications protocol and toolset that enables apps built on the Ethereum protocol stack to talk to each other. It combines all the aspects of the distributed hash table and point-to-point communications system to allow apps on the

Ethereum system to communicate with one another.

- Swarm or Swarm Hash. Swarm or Swarm Hash is a peer-to-peer file sharing protocol that is designed to efficiently store and retrieve data for use in Ethereum apps and contracts. The simplest analogy to draw with Swarm would be that it is essentially the BitTorrent for Ethereum.

- Oracle. Ideally, we should have a construct that communicates the outside realities to the smart contracts. In Ethereum, the constructs that communicate with the external realities are called oracles. While some of the projects create private oracle systems, there have been attempts to develop a single system to help verify inputs to multiple Blockchains.

The third layer of the Ethereum technology stack is Dapps. Dapps can be formed from a single DAO or a series of DAOs that work in unison to create an application. This can result in something similar to Google Chrome or Microsoft Outlook. Such apps can be made to achieve a certain functionality

At the top layer or the application layer of the Ethereum stack technology is Mist. Mist provides users with the capability to explore the apps and offerings that utilize the Ethereum protocol. Designed as a distributed app discovery tool, Mist serves as a wallet for the smart contracts that enables GUI-allowing users to set their transaction fees and manage custom tokens dynamically.

Scripting language

A scripting language is simply a programming language that supports the development of scripts (programs that are designed for run-time environments and to minimize the need for human intervention). Due to this property, scripting languages are be best exploited for experimenting and rapid prototyping.

The Bitcoin system has a primary scripting language, and there's justification for this. From the beginning, Bitcoin's developers have always prioritized the capability to "push" movement of Bitcoin via the Bitcoin Blockchain rather than other applications. While discussions are at an advanced stage to incorporate a more powerful scripting language that promotes app development, the Bitcoin community has largely remained reluctant to embrace new functionalities.

In fact, the community has given credence to censorship resistance and network security at the expense of a more powerful scripting language that could enhance the development of apps. Ethereum, on the other hand, aims to be the "Turing-complete" system. This implies that, if any user has unlimited resources such as memory, computational power, and storage, then the infinite "loops" can be executed.

In other words, both the logic and functionality that can be incorporated in Ethereum transactions is only limited by the availability of the protocol currency. However, this feature comes at the cost of enhanced security. While powerful scripting enhances greater features, the additional tools also create new security challenges for the user.

Ethereum Transactions

The most notable difference between Bitcoin and Ethereum transactions is that Ethereum blocks contain both a transaction list and the most recent state of the ledger. This helps to manage two main types of accounts:

- ***Externally owned accounts (EOAs)***. EOAs interact with and generate regular updates on the Ethereum blockchain.
- ***Contracts***. Contracts programmatically execute only when they receive instructions, which are in the form of a transaction, from an EOA. The contracts can either push or pull funds and can also request these actions from other contracts while calling on the contract code to perform dynamic actions.

Ethereum doesn't use the transaction inputs or outputs, which departs from the Unspent Transaction Outputs (UTXO) model of the Bitcoin that was popularized by Satoshi Nakamoto. In the Bitcoin's model, each newly minted Bitcoin becomes an UTXO with the owner who retains the right to consume that Bitcoin in the future.

During any Bitcoin transaction, the UTXO becomes the input that is spent in the transaction. When these Bitcoins are consumed or pushed to another Bitcoin user, a brand new UTXO is generated. In contrast, Ethereum stores the current state of its network, including a full list of the accounts and their associated accounts' balances.

Rather than confirming that the UTXO spent in the transaction are valid, Ethereum network determines whether the sender has a sufficient account balance, just like a bank verifying whether a given check can be cleared. This feature becomes vital when the transactions include contacts as recipients. If the transaction recipient is also contracted, then that contract's piece of code will also be executed, changing both the state of that contract and triggering other contracts to execute codes as well.

The Ethereum Blockchain

Just like Bitcoin, the Ethereum ecosystem also operates global transaction of ledgers that achieves remote and distributed validation using a Proof-of-Work (PoW) protocol. The PoW is a consensus mechanism in which participants spend a significant amount of energy in identifying unique pieces of data that can be verified by the wider network.

This information is used to generate the blocks, or certain finite volumes of transaction data, which serve as a reference for other network participants. The resultant Blockchain can offer a history of the Ethereum network at each of these intervals, therefore generating a shared truth that relates to all transactions.

The blocks in both Bitcoin and Ethereum are similar in that they contain information such as the block number (which specifies the number of blocks that have passed since the initial block) and the difficulty (a metric that specifies how challenging it is to compute the work required to generate a block). On the Bitcoin ecosystem, the transaction script is stateless meaning that there is no state before the execution of the script. Any update to this state is not stored after its execution.

Contracts on the Ethereum system are considered stateful in the sense that they are aware of their past information that was stored on the network and when they are instructed to via smart contracts, they can then take action. In other words, these contracts can receive a block of data and run all the transactions to verify any mathematical figure representing the system state at that moment in time. If the network nodes can validate the data, then they will accept the block for inclusion on the Blockchain.

Block size, Blockchain size and Block Times

On the Bitcoin blockchain, the blocks are limited to 1 MB in size. This not only creates a caveat on the volume of transactions that can be processed within a given time, but it has also turned out to be a major point of disagreement within the Bitcoin community as to whether to stick to it or to increase the size.

Ethereum on the other hand has no such limit on the block size. This is necessary because Ethereum executes both the scripts and the contracts. Capping the block size would not only impede the concept of "Turing-completeness" but would also limit the volume of storage that a contract could use to execute.

Instead of restricting the size of its blocks, Ethereum utilizes a mechanism that makes contracts more expensive to implement when they are larger in size.

What about the Blockchain size?

The process of allocating the Blockchain size is akin to that of the Bitcoin network. The larger the number of transactions executed on Ethereum, the more data all the peers in the system will need to store. This is due to the fact that the need to keep track and store all these transactions requires resources from the network of computers that are running the Blockchain. As of May 2017, the size of the Ethereum blockchain has grown to approximately 11 GB.

While this is still smaller than the Bitcoin network's blockchain size of roughly 69 GB, it is worth noting that Bitcoin has been around for a longer time compared to Ethereum. Assuming an average growth rate of around 1 GB per month, the Ethereum's blockchain is still growing at snail's pace compared to Bitcoin's. However, Ethereum has gained significant grip since its genesis block. As the network becomes more popular, its monthly growth rate may increase.

When it comes to Block times, Ethereum is faster compared to Bitcoin. The block time has been set from 14 to 15 seconds using a Ghost protocol while that of Bitcoin is 10 minutes. Therefore, Ethereum transactions are faster when compared to Bitcoin transactions.

Consensus Algorithms

For any decentralized computing system to function properly, there must be some sort of mechanism by which the entire network can come to an agreement with its state, or how its token supply is divided among the registered nodes on the network.

The Bitcoin system uses what is commonly called "Nakamoto consensus." Indeed the radical innovation behind the Bitcoin technology, Nakamoto's invention solved a longstanding complex computer science problem that is commonly known as the Byzantine Fault Tolerance or Byzantine Generals' Problem.

It is conceptualized on the idea that one person can't trust another person who has the potential motivation to lie and one can't entirely trust the integrity of any given communication if it passes through a third-party. Bitcoin solves this task by creating a chain of proof of work. The miners on the Blockchain spend considerable amounts of energy to solve a complicated cryptographic algorithm in a bid to receive rewards when they find the next block in the Blockchain.

Since the next block always trails the previous block (implying that you start the algorithm from the point of the block), Bitcoin miners can rush to verify that the block is valid and proceed to find the next block so that they claim a reward. Ideally, mining is incentive compatibility, and the immutable nature of the entries in the Blockchain provides a solution to the Byzantine Generals' problem.

Even though plans are underway to migrate the Bitcoin network to a different protocol in the next few years, as of the time of writing, Ethereum still uses a similar PoW protocol that is known as Ethash. So, how is Ethash different from PoW?

In Bitcoin's PoW, the miner builds a candidate block that is filled with transactions. Once the candidate block is established, the miner calculates the hash function—the algorithm that determines the integrity of data—to determine if it can fit in the current target Blockchain. If the hash algorithm can't fit in the current Blockchain, it will automatically update the Blockchain by adding the transactions to it.

On the other hand, the Ethash uses different cryptographic primitive for its hashing function—SHA-3 or rather SHA-256 to verify the transactions on the Blockchain. While the differences are nuanced, Ethash has been designed to make Ethereum resistant to the high-powered mining chips that are currently dominating the Bitcoin industry.

It also makes it more accessible to "light" client implementations that enable users to use Ethereum without having to first to download the Ethereum blockchain to their devices. Today, the majority of Bitcoin mining is performed in data centers that are mostly VC-backed companies that manage the production cycle of the equipment and collaborative collections of individual miners that are commonly known as mining pools.

To mitigate this consolidation, Ethereum mining was set up so that it can only be performed with powerful GPUs. The network is permission-less, meaning that any node that purchases a GPU and decides to run an Ethereum client can start processing transactions. However, if the intended switch to the new "Proof-of-Stake" consensus algorithm occurs, mining may no longer be required in the near future.

Ethereum Mining

Ethereum mining is the process of using your computer to produce blocks that are used to verify and process the transactions that occur in Ethereum systems. The blocks that your computer produces contain data from other previous blocks. The process of creating these blocks is tedious and demands a lot of computer processing power.

Without an incentive, no user will bother wasting their time creating blocks in the Blockchain. Therefore, as an incentive, any person who generates a block successfully is rewarded.

Solo or pool mining?

Ethereum mining is very similar to real mining when you consider each GPU to be the user performing that mining.

Solo mining is when you mine the Ethers by yourself. The advantage of solo mining is that anything that you find is completely yours. Unfortunately, if you only have a few miners, it can take you a large amount of time to find that Ether. Besides, the frequency of getting the Ether can also vary greatly.

You can have a week where you hit the Ether thrice, but then nothing for a whole month. Obviously, if you have many miners—or GPUs for that matter—then the outcome will be more stable. However, any threshold that has a mining rate of less than 1GH/s isn't advisable if you are aiming for profitability. If you're not bothered about the shifts in which you find Ether, then solo mining may be a good option for a mining rate above 100Mh/s since you don't need to pay fees to anyone.

With pool mining, many miners—or GPUs—join forces to try and find Ethers. The Ethers found are then shared equally among the miners, even though some pools choose to distribute the rewards in the form of ratios depending on numerous factors. However, in pool mining, you are required to pay a small fee (generally less than 1% of the reward) to the pool operators for maintaining the mining service. The upside of pool mining is that you'll always have consistent payout and will therefore make more money.

Ethereum Basic Hardware and Software

Minimally, you'll need a computer (with a fast processing power), the application for mining the Ether and high-speed Internet connection. Below is a list of specifications for the hardware you will need:

- CPU. When selecting the CPU, you should go for the bare minimum. I don't recommend buying the cheapest computer. This is because extra processing power will be required to perform computations.

- RAM. You should have a computer with a bare minimum of 4GB. If you're going for solo mining, it's important to have as much RAM capacity as possible to boost your chances of success.

- GPU. Strictly speaking, GPU-mining in Ethereum is much faster compared to CPU-mining. Currently, CPU-mining is no longer profitable or worthwhile. Even entry-level GPU-mining is about 200 times faster than CPU-mining. Currently, RX480s are one of the most popular GPUs that you can find for Ethereum mining cards. Just ensure it has enough processing capabilities.

- Hard drive. For the hard disk, using an SSD is critical. While SSDs can be more expensive, you will only need around 16GB, which will cost you fewer dollars.

What about the software?

Each mining software that you find in the market has evolved over the years. However, some have developed more than others. The primary contenders for Ethereum mining are Geth, MinerGate, Claymore and Genoil.

Geth

Geth is the original software from the Ethereum Foundation team. If you want to solo mine, then Geth will be your best bet. It's simple and straightforward to use. It can also help you create your wallet. If you prefer the GUI option, you can try Mist/Ethereum Wallet.

MinerGate

MinerGate isn't the best bet if you're planning to have dedicated mining rigs. However, if you want to mine on an existing computer as a hobby, then it's perfect. While it takes a fee from your mining process, its GUI is fast and simple. It has some challenges that can encourage you to mine if you're a beginner.

Genoil

Genoil is improving continuously and optimized for Ethereum. It executes smoothly, and you can get up and running with it in. If you're only intending to mine Ethereum, then Ethminer by Genoil will be your strong bet.

Claymore

Claymore is easy to set up and has a ton of added functionalities, such as fan management, that are not present in other miners.

That said, it's important to note that there's a clear difference between Ethereum mining and mining Ethereum well. Most of the applications for mining Ether may carry out numerous calculations simultaneously.

The calculations of these applications may end up straining the performance of your computer. Therefore, before you make a decision as to whether you want to mine Ether or not, you should ensure that your computer has sufficient processing power capabilities.

It's also vital to note that Ethereum mining performance is usually measured in Hashes per second (Hash/s). A Hash per second simply refers to the number of times that the processor can convert the data that's supplied to blocks in one second.

Next up, let's explore the Ethereum mining tools.

Ethereum mining tools

Here are some of the Ethereum tools that you must have before you begin mining:

Ethereum Wallet

When you begin mining, you will need to store your Ether in a safe location. You can store your Ether in two ways, either using a local wallet or an online wallet. A local wallet has better safety since it will always remain under your control. However, if you use a local wallet, then you must either install it on a computer that's not your Ethereum miner or regularly transfer your funds elsewhere.

The main reason for this is that if your computer crashes, it may be difficult to recover any Ether that is kept on it.

Mist / Ethereum Wallet

Both the Mist and the Ethereum Wallet are official developments by the Ethereum Foundation team. While at the heart of it, these two systems are straightforward to use and pack a lot of extra features. As it is integrated with ShapeShift, it will allow you to accept payments from Bitcoin and other alternative crypto currencies. If you're interested in building smart contracts, then Mist/Ethereum Wallet is your best bet.

Geth (with Etherwall)

Geth is the underlying program code for the Mist wallet and is the primary service for syncing the Ethereum Blockchain. Unfortunately, it uses commands that are typed on command prompt, making it challenging and annoying to use. Geth (with Etherwall) incorporates GUI front-end to it, making it easier to use.

My EtherWallet

MyEtherWallet is an open source and client-side Ether wallet that runs on JavaScript. It makes it easy to build secure wallets without using the command line or executing an Ethereum client on your computer. When you run MyEtherWallet on an offline computer, you can easily develop secure paper wallets for your Ether holdings.

Poloniex and Kraken

Poloniex and Kraken are online crypto currency trading platforms. You can use the deposit address at Poloniex and Kraken to transfer any Ether that you make directly.

Setting up the mining process

When it comes to selecting your Ethereum mining OS platform, there are three main contenders: Windows OS, Linux OS, and ethOS. Let's jump in and explore how the process of setting up Ethereum on these platforms.

Mining Ethereum on Windows OS

Here are the steps that you can follow to mine Ether on a Windows OS:

- Download the **Geth** software application. Geth is an application that acts as an interface between your computer and the Ethereum network.
- Unzip the Geth file on your computer.
- Run the application that you've just downloaded. To execute the program that you've just downloaded, type in the search button the keyword "cmd" and click on it.
- Once the command prompt is opened, type in "cd /" to navigate to "C :\>."
- Create a new account by typing "*geth account new*" at the command prompt and press the

enter key. You should have a screen similar to the one below:

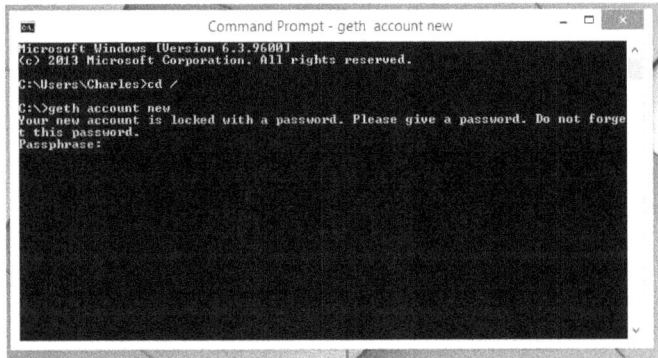

- Type in the password that you'll be using on your Ethereum network
- Let the Geth application begin communicating with the rest of Ethereum system. To achieve this, type in "geth -- rpc" at the command prompt and press the enter key. You should see a screen similar to the one below:

- Wait for the Ethereum Blockchain to complete downloading and synchronizing with the Ethereum system.

- Download and install the Ethminer application. The Ethminer allows your CPU to run hashing algorithms in a fast and secure manner.

- Open another command prompt and navigate to "C:\Program Files" by typing the "cd" command at the command prompt.

- While in "C:\Program Files," type "cd Ethereum 1.0.1\Release" and press the enter key where 1.0.1 is the version of the Ethereum miner. Of course, you'll have to confirm this first.

- Now type "ethminer –G" at the command prompt and press the enter key. Wait for the mining process to start. The DAG file will be created within 10 minutes. You should now see a screenshot similar to the one below:

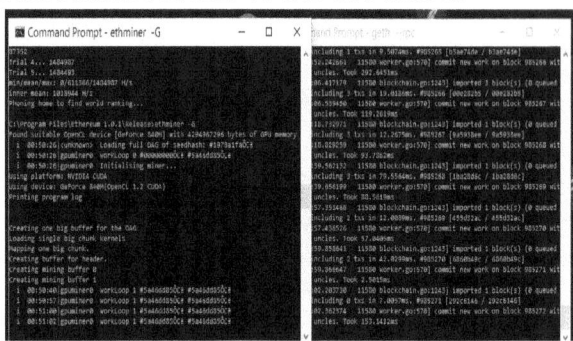

Mining Ethereum on Linux OS

Here are the steps that you can use to mine Ethereum on Linux OS:

1. **Step one**: Ensure that you have installed and updated your AMD Driver to the latest version. You can now download the AMDGPU-Pro driver, unzip it and install it.
2. **Step two**: Install the Ethereum Software. To install the Ethereum client, you will need to add the repository. If you're using a Debian-based Linux distribution, such as Ubuntu, type the following commands at the command prompt of your Terminal:

```
sudo apt-get install software-properties-common

sudo add-apt-repository ppa: ethereum/ethereum
sudo apt-get update
```

If you're using a CentOS/Redhat OS, such as Fedora, type the following commands at the command prompt of your Terminal:

```
sudo yum install software-properties-common

sudo add-yum-repository ppa: ethereum/ethereum
sudo apt-get update
```

3. **Step three:** Now install your preferred Ethereum software by typing the following commands at the command prompt if you're using a Debian-based Linux distribution OS:

```
sudo apt-get install ethereum
```

```
sudo apt-get install ethminer sudo apt-get install
geth
```

If you're using a CentOS/Redhat OS, type the following commands at the command prompt of your Terminal:

```
sudo yum install ethereum
sudo yum install ethminer sudo apt-get install geth
```

Mining Ethereum on Mac OS

Homebrew is by far the easiest way to install go-ethereum in Mac OS. If you haven't installed it on your system, install it first. To set up Ethereum on your Mac OS, follow the steps outlined below:

- Run the following commands to install geth:
```
brew tap ethereum/ethereum
brew install ethereum
```
- You can now install the develop branch by running the following commands:
```
brew install ethereum --devel
```
- Now, run the new geth account to create an account on your node.

Ethereum mining profitability calculator

Now that you have set up your Ether and you're ready for mining, what's next?

It's now time to start reaping from your investments in Ethereum. But not that fast. How do you determine if mining the Ethers is profitable or not? That's where the Profitability Calculator comes in. The Ethereum mining profit calculator can help you find out if mining Ether will be profitable. The Ethereum Profitability calculator provides an estimate of the expected crypto currency earnings based on statistical calculations.

These statistical computations are done using the values entered and doesn't account for the difficulty and exchange rate fluctuations, the stale or rejected rates, and the mining pool's efficiency. If you are mining using the pooling system, the estimated expected Ethereum earnings can vary depending on the pool's efficiency, stale rates and the fees charged. On the other hand, if you are mining using the solo approach, the estimated expected crypto currency earnings can vary depending on your luck and the stale or rejected rate.

For help with some of the calculations Ethereum miners need to make, there are many sites that provide Ethereum profitability calculators. In all these calculators, all you need is to input parameters such as how much your equipment cost, hash rate, power consumption, and the current Ethereum price to see how long it will take to have a higher ROI.

Ethereum Virtual Machine (EVM)

The source code for Bitcoin was implemented in C++. Therefore, the limited scripting for Bitcoin apps often happens at a more granular layer. The net effect of granular programming is that it makes the platform less desirable for the development of many new-age web-based systems. However, the high-level languages that are readily available within the Ethereum ecosystem make smart contracts accessible to most developers.

For instance, Geth—which is implemented in Go— is available to Ethereum developers and can be used to encode complex smart contracts in a simplified manner using the EVM. In other words, Ethereum is a more expanded form of Bitcoin built not just as a crypto currency system but with smart contracts in mind. That's why any developer interested in the future development of smart contracts should consider understanding the EVM.

But what is the Ethereum Virtual Machine?

Ethereum is a programmable Blockchain system. Rather than just providing you with a set of pre-defined operations—like those in Bitcoin transactions—Ethereum allows you to develop your own apps of any magnitude and complexity. In particular, Ethereum serves as a digital platform for the development of decentralized apps, including, but not limited to crypto currency systems.

Ethereum was invented with smart contracts in mind. At the heart of Ethereum is the Ethereum Virtual Machine which is simply abbreviated as EVM. EVM can execute the smart contract code of any arbitrary algorithmic length and complexity. In technical terms, EVM can be perceived as a complete "Turing machine".

The Turing machine can be perceived as a "world computer" that any developer can create and run apps on using a friendly programming language. For instance, you can create smart contracts and execute them on EVM using programming languages such as Python, Go and JavaScript. Sounds interesting, isn't it?

Now, just like any Blockchain-based system, Ethereum also uses a peer-to-peer network protocol where the Blockchain database is supported and updated by multiple autonomous nodes that are connected to the Blockchain network. Each node of the Blockchain network must run the EVM and execute the same smart contract instructions.

Now, to begin developing your smart contracts, you'll need a client that connects to the Ethereum network. In particular, the client will serve as your window to the distributed Blockchain network and provide you with a view of the Blockchain—where the EVM has been installed.

You can use Solidity, Serpent or Pyethereum platforms to execute your smart contracts. Let's jump in and explore these platforms.

Solidity

Undoubtedly, Ethereum would be incomplete without a native programming language. That language is none other than Solidity. Solidity is the code that allows

Ethereum developers to run contracts and programs in a decentralized manner. It resembles the browser-based JavaScript language but is instead used for running Ethereum smart contracts.

In contrast to Object-oriented languages such as Java and JavaScript (that combines variables, data, and functions to execute certain human-operated commands), Solidity is a "contract-oriented" language. Its run-time environment tasks are all automated and the objects are bundled together to eliminate the need for manual commands.

It is often described as the Ethereum's scripting language. However, it is actually a compiled language and not a scripting language. It compiles the smart contract instructions into bytecode so that the EVM can read them. This is a vital feature of contracts since they are not independent programs but rather partially compiled codes that rely on EVMs to run.

Solidity has also been designed to express agreements that can encode relationships and arguments that usually exist in real life. Therefore, it includes more concepts than an Object-Oriented language. The identity, ownership and protection often form a core component of the programming grammar.

As the programming language matures and adds more libraries and users, it has the promise to create massive and powerful constructs that may end up having real-world applications, such as IoT devices.

Serpent

The serpent is one of the high-level programming languages that are used to write Ethereum smart contracts. The serpent is designed to be similar to Python. It is intended to be optimally clean and straightforward by combining many of the efficiency benefits of low-level language with ease-of-use in its programming style.

At the same time, it adds unique domain-specific features for smart contract programming. The current version of the Serpent compiler, which is available on GitHub, is written in C++, enabling it to be easily incorporated in any client. In addition to providing efficiency while programming, Serpent has the following key distinctions when compared to Python:

- While Python integers have an unlimited size, the Serpent integers go up to 2256.
- While Python program allows decimals, Serpent doesn't support decimals.
- Python compiler supports lists, dictionaries, and other advanced data structures while Serpent has no list comprehensions.
- Python compiler supports first-class functions while Serpent doesn't.

Pyethereum

Pyethereum is the Python core library for implementation of Ethereum smart contracts. It provides the basic classes and necessary routines for interacting with Ethereum smart contracts. We have made a virtual machine that contains all the necessary software. In particular, Pyethereum allows you to program, letting you interact with the Blockchain to test and run your smart contracts.

Pyethereum is a Python-based Ethereum client system. But it's not the only one available. Today, there are Ethereum implementations in C++ (CPP-ethereum) as well as Go (go-ethereum or simply Geth). At the most basic level, you can begin using Pyethereum, which is the latest OS (whether Windows, Linux or Macintosh), and the most recent version of Serpent.

Ethereum Supporting Protocols

Besides the main Ethereum Blockchain protocol, other supporting technologies in the Ethereum development seek to complement the network, making the Ethereum components run more efficiently.

For instance, a whole new set of protocols is currently being developed to increase the functionality of the decentralized applications while tools keep on evolving to allow the programs to harness data from multiple Blockchains. While there may be a few protocols that unite the Ethereum concepts on the surface, all are aimed at making the Ethereum more flexible for developers and users.

Here are some of the most common supporting protocols:

Whisper

Whisper is a communications protocol and toolset that enables apps built on the Ethereum protocol stack to talk to one other. It combines all the aspects of the distributed hash table and point-to-point communications system to allow apps on the Ethereum system to communicate with one another.

For instance, the whisper protocol can facilitate the exchange of data by buying and selling offers to provide seamless communications akin to that of chatroom-like apps. You can think of Whisper as an Ethereum app for whistleblowers who have a trove of data stored and may want to communicate to a journalist, but he/she doesn't want his/ her identity to be linked to the data.

Swarm

Swarm—or SwarmHash as it is commonly known as—is a peer-to-peer file-sharing protocol that is designed to store and retrieve data efficiently for use in Ethereum apps and contracts. The simplest analogy to draw with Swarm would be that it is essentially the BitTorrent for Ethereum.

There is no doubt that to store data directly on the Ethereum Blockchain would be expensive. While the contract code is to be kept on the Blockchain, any reference data that is needed for contract execution should not. For example, if a simple, smart contract were to say deliver an e-card with the pictures, the photos would take up a vast volume of space.

Perhaps a school may want to send out an album with photos of its graduating class. If such an application runs on Ethereum, it might demand a contract that is 1 KB but is designed to deliver approximately 1 GB of data. Storing and transacting a 1 KB of code can cost users a few dollars, whereas storing the album itself will always cost more.

By storing the album remotely and accessing the file using a BitTorrent-like system such as Swarm, it would allow Ethereum apps to deliver the instructions, alongside the files to be transferred, using the Swarm system and not the Ethereum Blockchain.

Oracles

For Ethereum contracts to execute correctly, they need not just a well-designed series of "if ...then" statements, but also a method of determining the accuracy of the given inputs to those "if ...then" statements. Suppose it is raining in Singapore and several reliable sources can verify that it is raining, but how does Ethereum weed through possibly fraudulent sources to identify the accuracy of the input?

Ideally, we would have a construct that communicates the external realities to the smart contracts. In Ethereum, the constructs that describe the external realities are called oracles. While some of the projects are attempting to create their own private oracle systems, there have been attempts to develop a single system to help verify inputs to multiple Blockchains.

Even though at the moment, there are a limited number of data sources, developing a unified framework is achievable and can be cryptographically proven. In fact, it isn't difficult to figure out a future where smart technologies and the Internet of Things will allow all sorts of external data to be incorporated into the smart contracts.

Mist

If the Ethereum protocol is the new TCP/IP that promotes sharing of value as opposed to just storing information, the project needed for the new version of the browser that provides a useful frontend technology is definitely Mist. Mist provides users with capabilities to explore the apps and offerings that utilize the Ethereum protocol.

Styled as a distributed app discovery tool, Mist is designed to serve as a wallet for the smart contracts that enables GUI-allowing users to set their transaction fees and manage custom tokens dynamically.

Chapter 3

Ethereum Use Cases

The Ethereum technology is still at an infancy stage. Therefore, any business and technology enthusiasts who are interested in staying current on the implications of the technology should always track both technology and cases of its use in the industries. Below are some of Ethereum's use cases:

- Smart Contracts
- DAOs
- Dapps

Let's jump in and explore these use cases.

Smart Contracts

Smart contracts are self-executing algorithmic codes that are stored and replicated on a distributed ledger system—the Blockchain. The algorithm is executed by a network of nodes that run the Blockchain and can result in regular updates of the ledger. In other words, a smart contract is a program that executes on the Blockchain if an action is triggered.

For the program to run, it has to be verified by many nodes in the distributed network to ensure that it's trustworthy. If you were thinking about the Blockchain technology and its power of distributed reliable storage, then smart contracts have the potential to provide trustworthy computations on the distributed storage.

With smart contracts, there's no need for a single source of control. Smart contracts use the Blockchain technology where several parties—autonomous computers—use consensus mechanism to constantly check and re-verify any updates to the ledger. This promotes transparency.

Since all the nodes in the Blockchain network are running the same code, with each verifying the other, smart contracts will be visible to all. Any node can look into a smart contract, and if it's satisfied with the logic, it can use it. On the other hand, if the node doesn't agree with the code, it doesn't run it. That's how transparency is promoted in smart contracts.

Smart contracts can provide benefits for a wide range of industries such as banks, healthcare providers, and insurance companies. When implemented properly, these organizations can benefit from reduced risks, real-time processing, accurate and verified transactions, fewer third-parties and lower costs.

Smart contracts can be deployed using the Solidity language or Pyethereum scripting languages. Smart contracts programmatically execute only when they receive instructions, which are in the form of a transaction from an EOA. The contracts can either push or pull funds and request these actions from other contracts while calling on the contract code to perform dynamic actions. Here is a sample of a smart contract code:

```solidity
pragma solidity ^0.4.0;

contract MySimpleStorage {

    uint storedData;

    function set (uint mydata) {

        StoredData = mydata;

    }

    function get () constant returns (uint) {

        return storedData;

    }

}
```

DAOs

While smart contracts on their own are fascinating, it is the concept of a vast number of unified contracts working together that showcases the extensiveness and potential value of Ethereum's technology.

Combined with DAOs (Distributed Autonomous organization) or DACs (Distributed Autonomous Corporation), smart contracts can promote enforcement of rules in the ecosystem.

Here's how the DAOs work:

- A group of nodes writes the smart contracts (codes) that will run the company or organization.
- There is the first funding period, where nodes add funds to the DAO by buying the tokens that represent ownership (this is called a crowd sale or Initial Coin Offering (ICO)) to provide it with the resources it requires.
- When the funding period ends, the DAO begins to function.
- Nodes can then make the proposals to the DAO on how to spend the funds, and the nodes which have been bought in can vote to approve the proposals.

At the moment, all the smart contracts that we have discussed are owned and executed by other accounts which we assume were humans. But there is no bias against the robots or other people in the Ethereum ecosystem. In particular, the smart contracts can create arbitrary actions just like any other account would.

They can own tokens, participate in the crowd sales, and even act as voting members of other contracts. The DAOs can facilitate such arrangements in the Ethereum ecosystem. The way this particular democracy function is that any smart contract code must have an owner that works as the administrator.

The Owner can add (or eliminate) voting members in the organization. Any member can make a proposal to the ecosystem, which is in the form of a contract transaction to either send the Ether or execute some smart contract. The members can then vote to support or reject the proposal. Once a predetermined time is chosen and sufficient members have voted, the contract counts the number of votes and if there are enough, it will execute the given transaction.

Dapps

The primary objective of the Ethereum network is to serve as a platform for the development of Distributed applications (Dapps). Dapps can be developed from a single DAO or a series of DAOs that work in unison to create an application. This can result in something similar to apps such as Google Chrome or Microsoft Outlook.

Such apps can be made to achieve a particular functionality. However, for an application to be considered a Dapp, it must meet the following criteria:

- It must be completely open-source and operate autonomously with no entity managing the majority of its tokens. The app may adapt its protocol in response to the proposed improvements and market the feedback but all changes must be decided by consensus of its users.
- Its data and records of operation must be cryptographically stored in public. Blockchain must also be distributed to avoid any central points of failure.
- It must use cryptographic tokens to access the app, and any contribution of value from the miners should be rewarded in app tokens.
- It must generate tokens according to a standard cryptographic algorithm that acts as proof of the value.

Dapps are grouped into four categories:

- Smart contract services, utilities, and analytics
- Information validation and Oracle services
- Gambling and games
- Registry and corporate governance.

Chapter 4

Profit With Ethereum

It is true Ethereum, and its underlying Blockchain technology that has caught the investors' interest in Ether. This chapter explores the investment basics of Ethereum and its applicability to miners to provide you with the big picture that you will need before investing in Ethereum. Before we delve deeper into Ethereum investment, it is vital that we answer the question, "What is Ether"?

The concept of Ether

Ether—or ETH—is the unit of account and store value on the Blockchain of records in the Ethereum network. It is the equivalent of bitcoins (BTC) on the Bitcoin network. While having an economic value (in the sense that it is a scarce commodity), Ether is not meant to be used as an alternative currency like the Bitcoin.

Instead, it has been designed as a system reserve that powers the development of those seeking to use the Ethereum platform to create applications that can generate value for the users. If Bitcoin's value is obtained from the scarcity of the commodity and the security of the network, then Ether has value since it is required to execute scripts and smart contracts on the Ethereum ecosystem.

For this reason, Ether is now known as the "digital oil" while Bitcoin is the "digital gold". While bitcoin succeeded in proliferating naturally over time via Bitcoin mining, the Ethereum community wanted to find a way to kick-start the mining process and attract a base of Ethereum technology enthusiasts who could help the system to grow.

To reach a critical mass of Ethereum developers, Ethereum's team used Ether as a motivation to bring the project to life. In July 2014, Ethers became directly available for purchase on Ethereum.org and more than $18M was raised through that effort. The point of contention that has emerged in recent times hinges on the legality of the initial sale.

However, it is vital to note that to date, no action has been taken against any of the individuals or groups that were involved as well as other Blockchain development users that have used this approach to community building. Nonetheless, the legal technicalities involved have been acknowledged by Ethereum developers.

Inflation Rate

The Ethereum system has a mechanism for releasing new Ethers into the network over a given time. Something of significance to investors that are familiar with Bitcoin and other crypto currencies is that there is a difference between the approach in the Ethereum system and other crypto currency systems. For instance, in the Bitcoin network, the limit of all the bitcoins that will ever exist has been set at 21M

Bitcoins, a caveat that will require a consensus of nodes to change.

Ethereum, on the other hand, has no fixed limit on how much of its digital tokens will exist in the future. Instead, its development team wants to use its token system in a manner that encourages access by introducing 18M Ethers every year through mining. They argued that over a given time, this steady rate of inflation would decrease as the overall token supply increased.

As a result of inflationary rates, new participants in the ecosystem will be able to buy the new Ether or mine for the new Ether whether they are living in the year 2020 or 2120.

Similarly, the economic model of Ethereum is slightly different from that of Bitcoin as Ethereum does not halve the financial rewards after four years. This means that you'll receive the same amounts of Ether each year. However, in Bitcoin, the economic returns are halved after every four years. When it comes to reserve side of the digital currency, there's no limit in

Ethereum. In fact, the amount of Ether that can be circulated is limitless.

Gas

If Ether is operated as a way to allow access to Ethereum's world computer and guarantees its functionality, an economic structure is also required to limit access. To complement Ether and better explain the workings of its token, Ethereum introduced the concept of "Gas," a throttling approach that controls (in real time) how much Ether each smart contract costs.

Gas has a stable value that is presently set at 10 "Szabo", with one Ether being made up of 1M Szabo. The longer it takes for the smart contract to run, the more systematic resources it needs, thus requiring more fuel to execute the smart contract. Executing smart contracts based on the Ether limit or the Gas throttle is a market-based solution that instantaneously restricts the potential for system hackers to spam the network and reduces the need for setting a fixed size for new transaction blocks.

Ethereum Trading

How does Ethereum trading resemble in practice? Given that Ethereum is a public valued utility, answering this question requires well-designed and thought-out principles of data analysis. At the outset, you should understand the current state of the Ethereum project, how the marketplace is growing and the progress that is being made by the core development team.

Let's begin with the price.

Price

It is a fact that there is no true value that you can assign to any digital asset. The Ethereum trading system provides clarity as to what the users and traders believe is the value of the Ether. This metric can also be argued to be an indication of the overall confidence in the Ethereum project.

As an investment, Ether has demonstrated similar development as that of Bitcoin currency. At the time of Ethereum's first crowd sale, users were able to buy 2000 Ether with 1 BTC and that was trading for just over $600. Since then, Ether has witnessed its price rise and fall. Of particular significance is the fact that speculators always seem to be attracted to the coordinating action around major Ethereum project releases.

Still, such sliding movements have been trivial compared to Ether's overall price appreciation. At the time of the crowd sale, the price of 1 Ether was roughly $0.30. Compared to its value of $14.30 at the time writing this book, this denotes a 4,666% increase in value. An analysis of the Ethereum network's Blockchain shows that business is today pushing the majority of volumes, though how much could be specified as hypothetical is uncertain.

Ethereum Wallet

The first step towards getting started with Ethereum is setting up the wallet. Just like a real wallet where you store notes and coins, an Ethereum wallet lets you store your Ether. An Ethereum wallet is simply a file that you create for storing your Ether—the same way you would create a bank account to keep your money.

The wallet you create can be stored on different computers or devices (remember, Ethereum is a distributed system). Therefore, you can duplicate the wallet file. The wallet file comprises of two main parts namely: the file—which stores your Ether—and the wallet application—the program that opens the file on your computer.

Now, how can you set up a wallet file on your computer?

Well, you must have Bitcoin. This is because it's difficult to buy Ether using a credit card whereas the process of exchanging Bitcoins with Ether is relatively straightforward. Simply put, you need an official Ethereum wallet and Bitcoin that contains some coins for you to get started. Do keep in mind that both wallets must be up-to-date.

What happens when you create an account?

Every account that you create is defined by two keys namely, the Private Key and the Public Key. At this stage, it's important to note that both the private and public keys are simply encryption algorithms that are used to secure your account whenever you perform any transaction. Both keys are stored as a single file.

Conversion from Bitcoins to Ether

To convert from Bitcoins to Ether, follow the steps below:

- Log on to Poloniex.com and create an account.
- Log into your account.
- Click on the "BALANCES" tab and select the "DEPOSITS & WITHDRAWALS" link.
- Use the search button to find the Bitcoin's address.
- Copy the Bitcoin address and return to the Coinbase.
- Send the Bitcoins that you would like to invest in Ethereum.
- Wait for the transaction to be completed.
- Click on the "ETH" market and type in the amount of Ether that you would like to buy.

Ethereum security

It's your responsibility to look after your digital money. In fact, there are no built-in back apps that can help restore your Ether if something goes wrong. Therefore, it's vital to keep your wallet secure, backed up and in sync with the Blockchain.

Remember that every wallet that you create has two keys: the Private Key and the Public Key. The main function of these keys is to help with the encryption of transactions that take place online so that even if third-party persons intercept them, they will have a difficult time cracking and finding out what's being sent across the network.

Both Private and Public keys stored as a single file. The first rule for establishing a secure Ethereum system is knowing where the file is stored. In most systems, the key store file would be found in the key store subdirectory of the Ethereum's data directory. Of course, this depends on the type of OS that you're using.

Let's find out how different OS access this file.

#1: Windows OS

If you are running a Windows OS (any version), then the node's key store data directory will be located at:

C:\Users\username\%appdata%\Roaming\Ethereum.

You should replace the username with your name in order for you to access the key store file. For instance, if your name is Peter, then you can navigate to

C:\Users\peter\%appdata%\Roaming\Ethereum   to locate the key file.

#2: Linux OS

If you're running a Linux OS, then you can access the key store file at the following location:

Linux: ~/.ethereum

For you to access this file, all you have to do is to open the Terminal. Ensure that you have administrative privileges to access the file—use the su command and type your root password. After that, simply type ~/.ethereum and you'll access the key store file.

#3: Mac OS

For Mac OS, the key store will be found in the following path:

~/Library/Ethereum

Note that the path to the key store file will always be hidden from users. Therefore, you should use an appropriate method—that's allowed for your OS—to unhide the files.

Chapter 5

Ethereum Key Players and Technical Infrastructure

The technical infrastructure of the Ethereum project mirrors the core ethos of the project itself by being widely decentralized. The Ethereum project is a massive undertaking, led primarily by its developers, but also depends on the distributed efforts of its diverse community. The key players in this industry are:

- Developer Leads
- The Ethereum Foundation
- Decentralized Projects
- Ethereum startups

Let's explore these players.

Developer Leads

Members of the Ethereum community generally incline towards being elusive when discussing its early history and growth even though it's an open secret that there have been several changes to its membership. For instance, the original thread that introduced the Ethereum project on the Bitcoin Talk online forum has been modified since its original publication, with the full list containing the names of the developers and architects who have since shifted onto other projects.

A major distinction with Bitcoin is that while the Bitcoin creator—Satoshi Nakamoto—abandoned the project at an infancy stage, Ethereum has undoubtedly been fueled by the active involvement of its inventor, Vitalik Buterin, and the core development team. Two of the core developers within the Developer Leads that are often cited are Gavin Wood (formerly the project's lead C++ developer) and Jeffrey Wilcke (the lead Golang developer). Other prominent developers include the many people employed by the Ethereum Foundation.

The Ethereum Foundation

The leading firm behind the Ethereum project is the Ethereum Foundation. Established as a non-profit making organization in June 2014 in Switzerland, the Ethereum Foundation has made concerted efforts to help drive its growth by incorporating innovative approaches towards development.

Its membership comprises of the following:

- Vitalik Buterin, the creator of Ethereum.
- Gavin Wood, formerly the project's lead C++ developer.
- Jeffrey Wilcke, its lead Golang developer.
- Bernd Lapp
- Stefano Bertolo
- Yessin Schiegg
- William Mougayar

Decentralized Projects

The Ethereum project has already seen the emergence of several projects that seek to bring its central concepts to life. Among these projects are:

- The DAO
- The Augur

Startups

Even though the Ethereum project is still in its early stages, the first wave of Ethereum projects is being observed with keen interest by venture capital firms that have expertise in the Blockchain domain. Among the Ethereum startups are:

- Backfeed
- BlockApps
- Ether.camp
- Ethcore
- Otonomous
- Akasha
- Colony
- ConsenSys
- Plex.ai
- Provenance
- Slock.it

Chapter 6

The Future of Ethereum

The Blockchain technology exposed the world to the concept of trustless data structures, giving us a glimpse of the future with the launch of the Bitcoin crypto currency. The Bitcoin crypto currency system has indeed changed the currency landscape. However, its key challenges have forced key developers to rethink its model and focus on the more open source, scalable and innovative Ethereum technology.

Surely, the Ethereum technology has given us a glimpse of a better future. Iteratively, it is a remarkable step forward, but we aren't there yet. This has been possible because of the Ethereum's underlying technology. However, the current consensus algorithm—the PoW—has hampered the growth of Ethereum technology.

The shift from PoW to PoS in the future could significantly reduce the computational load of the network, making Ethereum technology more effective and efficient. The distributed storage solutions and the state channels could also substantially increase its capabilities. Right now, the solutions provided by the ubiquitous Blockchain technology and the Ethereum system are still under development. As such, they may not come to their envisioned fruition.

- As competition amongst organizations in many industries stiffens, the Blockchain technology is likely to become even more in-demand in the future.

   While there are several competing Blockchain systems out there, with the backing of the tech-enthusiasts and companies, it stands to reason that the Ethereum project could become the go-to as more businesses seek to include the technology in their operations.

CONCLUSION

The Bitcoin technology exposed the world to the concept of trustless data structures, giving us a glimpse of the future. Surely, the Ethereum technology has given us that view of a better future. Iteratively, it is a remarkable step forward, but we aren't there yet. This has only been possible because of Ethereum's underlying technology.

The Blockchain technology has become increasingly popular in the past few years, but many tech enthusiasts are still not sure exactly what it is. Right now, the solutions provided by the ubiquitous Blockchain technology and the Ethereum system are still under development. As such, they may not come to their envisioned fruition.

Can the Ethereum project navigate this potential fork in the road and the myriad of challenges ahead? While the future is forever uncertain, the real question is that in Ethereum's case, will it really be ethereal, or will it adapt the needs of the real world. My best bet is that Ethereum will indeed navigate these challenges and become "The Next Internet."

FURTHER RESOURCES

Below is a list of websites for useful Ethereum resources:

- www.coindesk.com
- www.cio.com
- www.investopedia.com
- www.daos.com
- www.ethereum.com
- www.github.com
- www.ethdocs.org
- www.vanderwijk.info
- https://medium.com/@ConsenSys/a-101-noob-intro-to-programming-smart-contracts-on-ethereum-695d15c1dab4
- http://cse.seu.edu.cn/people/zhchong/public/ReadingList/0.%20ethereum-homestead.pdf

NOTES

Chapter 1

1) http://media.coindesk.com/uploads/2017/02/CoinDesk MediaKit2017.pdf
2) https://forum.daohub.org/uploads/default/original/2X/b/b583e2bb2e6998bfec40d488b1709deb53abdc4a.pdf

Chapter 2

1) http://www.the-blockchain.com/docs/Coindesk-State-of-the-Blockchain-Q3-2016.pdf

Chapter 3

1) http://media.coindesk.com/uploads/2017/02/CoinDesk MediaKit2017.pdf
2) https://medium.com/@ConsenSys/a-101-noob-intro-to-programming-smart-contracts-on-ethereum-695d15c1dab4

Chapter 4

1) www.ethereum.org
2) www.github.com
3) www.ethdocs.org

Chapter 5

1) http://media.coindesk.com/uploads/2017/02/CoinDesk MediaKit2017.pdf

2) https://forum.daohub.org/uploads/default/original/2X/
b/b583e2bb2e6998bfec40d488b1709deb53abdc4a.pd
f

Chapter 6

1) http://cse.seu.edu.cn/people/zhchong/public/ReadingLi
st/0.%20ethereum-homestead.pdf
2) http://media.coindesk.com/uploads/2017/02/CoinDesk
MediaKit2017.pdf

ABOUT THE AUTHOR

Victor Finch is a zealous enthusiast for the latest technology, innovative gadgets and financial subjects ranging from Fintech to stock trading. These interests strike a deep resonating chord in his passions. He is an entrepreneur, an IT consultant, and a part-time author.

Victor as a child was always fascinated with how things worked; breaking apart his childhood toys is a common sight. Victor always has some innovative workarounds or solutions for his friends or family's problems such as a stubborn laptop that just like to "sleep" and how to improve the quality of life for his family.

If you spot someone, penning down his thoughts while walking down the streets of New York. That could be our dear Victor. He is always intrigued by the latest creativities around and just wants to tinkle with them when he has some me time.

In his spare time, Victor likes to explore the world, read his favorite books, open his little notes and write his next best selling book.

Victor's Message

Thank you for purchasing and reading my book! One of my passions is exploring potential investments opportunities and ethereum has such great potential. I hope you think so too and have found the answers you need to familiarize with the basic understanding on Ethereum and options that are available for your further exploration.

If you would like to read more great books like this one, why not subscribe to our website.

Thanks for reading! Please add your short review on Amazon

and let me know what your thoughts! – Victor

Other Victor's Titles You Will Find Useful

Blockchain Technology

Blockchain is a revolution that you should not ignore anymore.
Imagine you are been presented with an opportunity before the flourishing of Internet, what would you do? Now is the time!

THE ESSENTIAL QUICK & EASY BLUEPRINT TO
UNDERSTAND BLOCKCHAIN TECHNOLOGY AND
CONQUER THE NEXT THRIVING ECONOMY!
GET YOUR FIRST MOVER ADVANTAGE NOW!

—— VICTOR FINCH ——

https://www.amazon.com/dp/B01N1X3C75/

- You will understand everything you need to know about the mechanics of Blockchain.
- You will learn how you can benefit from Blockchain
- You will learn the legal implications of Blockchain technology

Victor Finch

ISBN: 978-1-5413-6684-8   Paperback: 102 Pages

eBook, Audiobook Available

Bitcoin

Are you still wondering or clueless about what is Bitcoin? Do you know Bitcoin is thriving robustly as a digital currency because of its characteristics for more than 8 years.

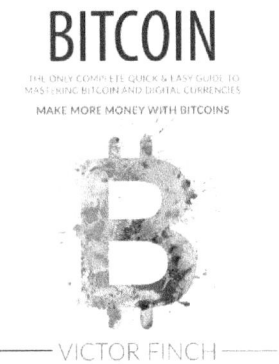

https://www.amazon.com/dp/B06XF6JK96/

- You will understand everything (including merits & demerits) you need to know about Bitcoin
- You will learn how to use Bitcoin and read the transactions.
- You will learn discover the best practices in using Bitcoin securely.

Victor Finch

ISBN: 978-1-5441-4139-8   Paperback: 98 Pages

eBook, Audiobook Available

Smart Contracts

Smart Contract is about the revolutionary (Blockchain Technology) approach with legal contracts or any legal agreements. This book offers an unprecedented peek into what the future may be like that could possibly change and enhance the traditional way of doing things for the better (many benefits).

https://www.amazon.com/dp/B06XW4L48F/

- You will learn how disruptive (positive) are Smart Contracts
- You will learn about the legal perspectives of Smart Contracts.
- **BONUS Highlight:** More than 7 Possible Smart Contract Use Cases in different industries.

Victor Finch
ISBN: 978-1-5446-9150-3   Paperback: 106 Pages
eBook, Audiobook Available

Data Analytics For Beginners

Leading companies must not only compete on faster ROI within the shortest time but also face stiff competition in this challenging digital frontier. Time is precious and marketing effort is worthless without information knowledge and precision execution. Data Analytics is your answer

https://www.amazon.com/dp/B071FM45GV/

- You will be expose to the big picture of Business Intelligence Data Analytics and its competitive advantages
- You will what is data mining in details and how can it work for you
- You will have a practical introduction on the four important steps in Data Analytics and explore the data analytics patterns

Victor Finch

ISBN: 978-1-5466-4191-9   Paperback: 127 Pages

eBook, Audiobook Available

Other Titles You Will Find Useful

Python

Python is a highly sought after skillset by many corporations. Possibilities with Python are limitless and often prefer over Java and C++ due to three characteristics that you will discover in this book.

https://www.amazon.com/dp/B06W2KKJK3/

- You will learn how to set up your first python.
- You will learn how to properly do error handling and debug to save you hours of time.
- BONUSES Included (plus Hands On Challenges)

Ronald Olsen

ISBN: 978-1-5426-6789-0   Paperback: 152 Pages

eBook, Audiobook Available

Python (Advanced)

Python (Advanced) is written for programmers, web developers, enterprise software engineers who seek to improve and enhance their programming skills with Python latest features, neat tricks that make your codes better, faster, lighter and more secure.

https://www.amazon.com/dp/B0732XKPSN/

- You will learn all about iterators, generators, descriptors and many more.
- You will explore all the important features that Python offers for advanced programmers.
- You will understand and learn how to use Python's powerful data analysis libraries that are making Python bypass R.
- BONUSES Included (plus Fun Hands On Challenges)

Ronald Olsen

ISBN: 978-1-5481-5643-5   Paperback: 142 Pages

eBook, Audiobook Available

Raspberry Pi

Raspberry Pi is a power minicomputer that has versatile uses and applications as such DIY security camera etc. The fun and innovative possibilities with Raspberry Pi is almost limitless and up to your imagination, knowledge and skills. This guide is suitable for beginners with no prior technical knowledge or skills required.

https://www.amazon.com/dp/B06XG1N4K3/

- You will learn the in and outs of Raspberry Pi 3
- You will learn how to set up Raspberry Pi 3.
- You will discover some of the fun, interesting and useful Raspberry projects

Ronald Olsen

ISBN: 978-1-5441-4145-9   Paperback: 102 Pages

eBook, Audiobook Available

AUVA PRESS

AUVA Press commits lots of effort in the content research, planning and production of quality books. Every book is created with you in mind and you will receive the best possible valuable information in clarity and accomplish your goals.

If you like what you have seen and benefited from this helpful book, we would appreciate your honest review on Amazon or on your favorite social media.

Your review is appreciated and will go a long way to motivate us in producing more quality books for your reading pleasure and needs.

Visit Us Online

AUVA PRESS Books

https://www.auvapress.com/books

Register for Updates

https://www.auvapress.com/vip

Contact Us

AUVA Press books may be purchased in bulk for corporate, academic, gifts or promotional use.

For information on translation, licenses, media requests, requests, please visit our contact page.

https://www.auvapress.com/contact

- END -